Try It! Math Problems for All

This is not your typical math book. Breaking away from the standard drill and practice routine, *Try It! Math Problems for All* is a collection of offbeat, open-ended math problems designed to make even the most math-averse student excited about working through these challenging yet accessible problems.

The 25 illustrated problems vary in difficulty, motivating students to think creatively on their own, or to engage in teamwork and cooperation within a group, while the Hints and Solutions section guides teachers to probe, suggest, and encourage students to explore even their most unusual insights on the way to a solution.

Perfect for any math classroom, club, after-school activity, or coaching session, *Try It!* celebrates not only the destination, but the journey, giving students a chance to relax, think differently, and, above all, have fun!

Optional Student Workbook Packs

In addition to this teacher's guide, companion student workbooks are available in packs of ten. The student workbooks feature ample room for student responses and notes, make reviewing and providing feedback on student work easier than ever, provide students with an easy-to-use reference to use during discussions, and save time, as there is no need to reproduce student handouts.

Jerry Kaplan is Professor Emeritus of Mathematics Education at Seton Hall University, where he taught for 28 years. He has written widely on many areas of teaching and learning mathematics, applying research to the practical needs of the mathematics curriculum and classroom, and is a strong advocate for including quality problems as an integral part of good math instruction.

Try It! Math Problems for All

Jerry Kaplan

Illustrated by Ysemay Dercon

Routledge
Taylor & Francis Group

NEW YORK AND LONDON

Designed cover image: Ysemay Dercon

First published 2024
by Routledge
605 Third Avenue, New York, NY 10158

and by Routledge
4 Park Square, Milton Park, Abingdon, Oxon, OX14 4RN

Routledge is an imprint of the Taylor & Francis Group, an informa business

© 2024 Jerry Kaplan. Illustrations © Ysemay Dercon

The rights of Jerry Kaplan to be identified as author of this work, and Ysemay Dercon to be identified as illustrator for this work, have been asserted in accordance with sections 77 and 78 of the Copyright, Designs and Patents Act 1988.

ISBN: 978-1-032-52419-1 (hbk)
ISBN: 978-1-032-51571-7 (pbk)
ISBN: 978-1-003-40659-4 (ebk)

DOI: 10.4324/9781003406594

Typeset in Bembo
by Deanta Global Publishing Services, Chennai, India

Contents

Try It! Math Problems for All: Photocopiable Problems   55

Preface

To students everywhere,

Hi, I am Jerry and I have a problem. In fact, I have 25 of them. Find one you like and **TRY IT!** That's right. **TRY IT!** We do not ask too much. Just **TRY IT!**

If you cannot figure it out, leave it alone. Then come back to it. Or try another one. And try some more. Speak to a classmate about it. Take your time. Some kids do not get it for a week. That's okay. This is not a race.

After a while, ask for help. A **hint**. Maybe another **hint**?

Try five different problems. Did it get any easier? Soon, you will have a favorite problem. Do not give up.

As a teacher, I spent years challenging students with problems. It started when I was a first-grade teacher. I asked my 19 students to figure out who was the oldest in the class. That took a month to figure out because first all the kids had to find out their exact dates of birth. Then we had to learn new stuff about calendars, years, months, weeks, and days. And finally, we wrote down the names of the oldest and youngest in the class with their birth dates. Later, we made a poster listing the whole class from youngest to oldest. I'll never forget the chatter from the kids about where they were on that list! Very exciting for all. And more: we made lists showing who was born in January, February, March, and so forth. I think I did more teaching in those four weeks than in any other four weeks of my teaching career!

From that experience I realized I wanted to use problem solving in all my classes. I did it later when I taught high school, and continued when I taught in college. Not only did my students have fun and a chance to work together, but students went home and tried our problems on family and friends. And came back to tell stories about all the trouble other folks had solving our problems!

What did you learn about how to solve problems?

First, take your time. **TRY IT!** and **TRY IT!** again. If you need a **hint**, ask for it. Or, try another problem. Another **hint**? Work on two at the same time. Keep thinking. After a while, you will learn you are better at solving problems than you thought! And that is a lot to learn.

Try It! Hints and Solutions

To teachers everywhere,

Try It! Hints and Solutions is a companion to **Try It! Math Problems for All**. It consists of many helpful hints and all the solutions for teachers to use in their classrooms. Beyond classrooms, **Hints and Solutions** is for anyone who wants to take a crack at the problems.

The problems. The purposes of the problems are to engage and challenge. We want to give students a break from the steady routine of drill and practice found in standard math lessons. But even more important, we want students of all backgrounds (and ages) to have a chance to think and grapple with an array of problems, whether alone or with others.

These problems are different from what you see in schools. They are not connected to the usual lessons or to the yearlong curriculum of any grade. Even more, they are not intended to be inserted at any specific time during the year. Simply stated, they are not aligned to any part of school teachings. Of course, that could be a stretch since with a bit of effort you can find a place and a time to insert a problem here or there in your normal program. We suggest that you don't. You will lose the spontaneity and the purpose of these problems.

When and where. Use them on special days. Use them early or late in the school year. Use them with one or more students. Small groups make sense. But above all give solvers time to think and brainstorm. Take the problems home? No problem. Remember, there is no clock such as "Your deadline is next Wednesday".

Start anywhere in the set. You will find easy and difficult problems next to each other. Encourage students to write their work down on paper. And when a student or a group has a solution, you may want to check it quietly. Eventually, you may want students to present their solutions to the class. Some teachers organize a REVEAL DAY for that purpose.

And for you. Have fun presenting problems to your groups – small, large, young, and old. Here is a chance to prod them forward as your audience starts to shout out

DOI: 10.4324/9781003406594-1

solutions. By throwing out hints and clues here and there, you encourage more probing. Do not give it away too soon. And above all have fun. Tease kindly. Play.

Background. We used these problems in courses at colleges and in many workshops with teachers and students from 5th to 12th grades. They are used today in schools by many teachers we know. We've presented them to people of all ages – and we all had fun. We continue to get positive feedback.

Be surprised. These problems are for all students, the high and low achievers, the quiet and loud ones. You probably know this: sometimes the quietest and the lowest performing students will surprise you if you give them a chance. They surprised us, for sure.

The accent is on **TRY IT!**

A Few Tips

We recognize that it is difficult to translate our personal tastes and styles for other teachers. But there are methods that, when timed correctly, will motivate your students, and encourage them to keep trying when solving problems. In the end, persistence by individuals and groups will solve problems and help to understand the "why" behind the solutions.

Here are a few tips on getting students engaged in solving problems.

- Encourage students to "throw out" ideas, that is, to brainstorm and talk to each other.
- Arrange groups so that students solve problems with other students.
- "Other students" can be one or as many as four or five students.
- If several groups are working at the same time, keep an eye on every group.
- Keep all students involved.
- Encourage students to explain to other students.
- Do not offer direct help, only tidbits of assistance.
- Above all, keep encouraging students throughout.
- Groups are not in competition; give different problems to different groups.
- Encourage students to write their ideas on paper.
- Above all, do not rush problem-solving sessions.

Organization of this Guide

We devote two pages to each problem: A **HINTS** page and a **SOLUTIONS** page. You will find all problems here exactly as you see them in the student workbook. **HINTS**: You will find the problem and several hints or prompts on how to get started on the problem.

- Make sure students understand the problem.
- Use these hints only after students understand the problem and had a chance to discuss it within their group.
- Offer hints only after students have made several attempts at solving and seem honestly stuck.
- The longer students struggle with finding a solution, the more they will learn from each other.
- Do not hint too early; that could impede those who are eager to figure things out on their own.
- Suggest that students take a break and come back to the problem later in the day or the next day.

SOLUTIONS: The problem is here again followed by a worked-out solution to the problem and the answer.

1 ADDING COINS TO A DOLLAR

a. Show how 50 US coins can add up to 1 dollar. Use pennies, nickels, dimes, and quarters.

b. Can you find another way to do this?

HINTS

The big picture: Which coins are we talking about? How much is each worth?

Get organized and make a chart.
Guess and check.
Try again.

1 ADDING COINS TO A DOLLAR

a.   **Show how 50 US coins can add up to one dollar. Use pennies, nickels, dimes, and quarters.**

b.   **Can you find another way to do this?**

SOLUTION 1

Coin	Value in cents (c)
Penny (p)	1
Nickel (n)	5
Dime (d)	10
Quarter (q)	25

Answer:

We need lots of pennies:

$$45\ p = 45\ c$$
$$1\ q = 25\ c$$
$$2\ n = 10\ c$$
$$\underline{2\ d = 20\ c}$$
$$50\ \text{coins} = 100\ c$$

SOLUTION 2

Answer:

$$40\ p = 40\ c$$
$$8\ n = 40\ c$$
$$\underline{2\ d = 20\ c}$$
$$50\ \text{coins} = 100\ c$$

2 COUNTING HANDSHAKES

a. You are one of ten students in an art class. If everyone shakes hands with everyone else, how many handshakes would there be?

b. If 20 students are in the class, how many handshakes would there be?

HINTS

Make sure all understand what a handshake is.
Select two students to illustrate a handshake.
Ask: How many handshakes for three people?

2 COUNTING HANDSHAKES

a. **You are one of ten students in an art class. If everyone shakes hands with everyone else, how many handshakes would there be?**

b. **If 20 students are in the class, how many handshakes would there be?**

SOLUTION

Start with 2 students and find how many handshakes. That is 1. Next, go to 3 students – that is 3 handshakes. 4 students – 6 handshakes. 5 students – the answer is 10 handshakes. Do you see a pattern? See chart below.

Number of students	Number of handshakes
2	1
3	3
4	6
5	10
6	15
7	?
8	?
9	?
10	?

Answer: The number of handshakes increases by the next whole number – 15, 21, 28, 36, **45**.

Extend the table to 20 students and you will get **190**.

3 PHONE

This is part of the keypad of a phone:

The numbers 3-2-7-6 spell the word FARM.

a. What numbers spell PURPLE?

b. What word do the numbers 6-2-8-4 spell? Can you get 2 words?

HINTS

Tell students to look at the keypad, then ask:

Which numbers spell CAT?

Which numbers spell DOG?

Which numbers spell MOON?

3 PHONE

This is part of the keypad of a phone:

The numbers 3-2-7-6 spell the word FARM.

a. **What numbers spell PURPLE?**

b. **What word do the numbers 6-2-8-4 spell? Can you get 2 words?**

SOLUTION

Answers:

- PURPLE = 7-8-7-7-5-3
- 6-2-8-4 spells MATH
- 6-2-8-4 spells OATH

4 SQUARES ON A CHECKERBOARD

How many squares are there in an 8 by 8 grid?

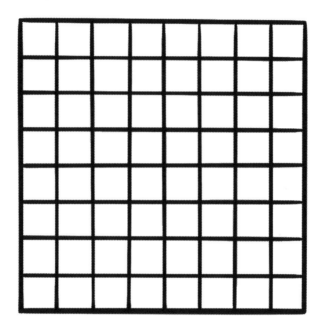

HINTS

Ask: How many squares do you see here?
(The answer is greater than 64.)

Do you see 5 squares here?

How many squares do you see here?

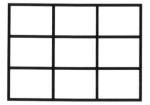

4 SQUARES ON A CHECKERBOARD

How many squares are there in an 8 by 8 grid?

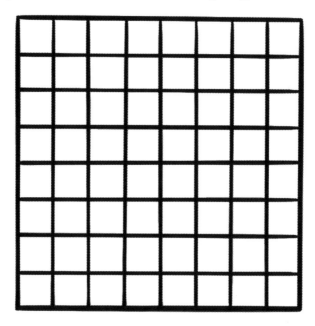

SOLUTION

Count squares of different sizes. Start with the smallest.

How many 1 by 1 squares, squares such as this one:

How many 2 by 2 squares, such as this one?

1 by 1s = 64 (8 across and 8 down)
2 by 2s = 49 (7 across and 7 down)
3 by 3s = 36 (6 across and 6 down)

Do you see the pattern?
Answer: Add: 64 + 49 + 36 + 25 + 16 + 9 + 4 + 1 = **204 squares**.

5 CUTTING A ROUND CAKE

Cut a round cake into eight equal parts with three cuts.

HINTS

Ask: Can you cut the cake into two equal parts?
Can you cut the cake into four equal parts?
What kind of cake is this?

5 CUTTING A ROUND CAKE

Cut a round cake into eight equal parts with three cuts.

SOLUTION

6 SHARING DONUTS

You and two friends have six donuts. In how many ways can you divide the six donuts so that each person gets at least one donut?

HINTS

Here's the start of the list. It shows three friends, A, B, and C, and the number of donuts.

A	B	C
1	1	4
1	4	1
4	1	1

6 SHARING DONUTS

You and two friends have six donuts. In how many ways can you divide the six donuts so that each person gets at least one donut?

SOLUTION

Continue making a list in a table:

A	B	C
1	1	4
1	4	1
4	1	1
1	2	3
1	3	2
2	1	3
2	3	1
3	1	2
3	2	1
2	2	2

Answer: There are ten ways to divide six donuts.

7 BACKWARDS AND FORWARDS

Write a five-letter word that spells the same word backwards and forwards.

HINTS

Think: which letters could be both at the beginning and the end? Here are a few:

M __ __ __ M

S __ __ __ S

T __ __ __ T

And many others.

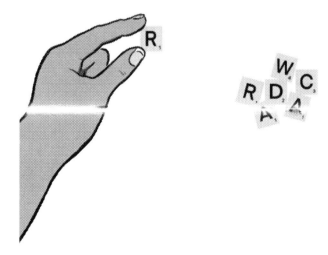

7 BACKWARDS AND FORWARDS

Write a five-letter word that spells the same word backwards and forwards.

SOLUTION

Answers:

MADAM
CIVIC
STATS
LEVEL
RADAR
TENET

8 HOW MUCH IS YOUR NAME WORTH?

Suppose A = $1, B = $2, C = $3, D = $4, and so forth.

Write your first name here. _____

How much is it worth? _____

Find a name equal to exactly $48.

HINTS

Make a chart of letter values:
A = $1, B = $2, C = $3, D = $4, and so forth.
Use trial and error. Try WILL = 23 + 9 + 12 + 12 = $56
Try CARMEN = 3 + 1 + 18 + 13 + 5 + 14 = $54
Keep trying.

8 HOW MUCH IS YOUR NAME WORTH?

Suppose A = \$1, B = \$2, C = \$3, D = \$4, and so forth.

Write your first name here. _____

How much is it worth? _____

Find a name equal to exactly \$48.

SOLUTION

Make a chart of letter values:
A = \$1, B = \$2, C = \$3, D = \$4, and so forth.
Try RON = 18 + 15 + 14 = \$47 ... almost.
Answer: TOM = 20 + 15 + 13 = \$48.
There are other names. Find one more.

9 COUNTING DIGITS IN A BOOK

The digits are 0, 1, 2, 3, 4, 5, 6, 7, 8, 9.

We write page numbers with digits: page 42, page 143.

a. **How many digits do we need to write for all pages from page 18 to page 32, including both pages 18 and 32?**

b. **How many digits do we need to write for all the pages from page 95 to page 112, including both page 95 and page 112?**

HINTS

Ask: How many pages between 1 and 5 including the first and the last page?
5 − 1 = 4 + 1 = 5 pages.
How many pages between 10 and 20 including the first and the last page?
20 − 10 = 10 + 1 = 11 pages.

Make sure these examples are clear.

9 COUNTING DIGITS IN A BOOK

The digits are 0, 1, 2, 3, 4, 5, 6, 7, 8, 9.
We write page numbers with digits: page 42, page 143.

a.   **How many digits do we need to write for all pages from page 18 to page 32, including both pages 18 and 32?**

b.   **How many digits do we need to write for all the pages from page 95 to page 112, including both page 95 and page 112?**

SOLUTIONS

Answers:

a. $32 - 18 = 14$ pages, then add 1 to include page 32. There are 15 pages. Each page uses 2 digits, so $15 \times 2 = 30$ digits. It takes 30 digits to write the pages from page 18 to page 32.

b.   Can we apply the same method to Part B? No, since not all pages require 2 digits as in Part A. First, find the number of digits for the pages with 2 digits – pages 95 through 99: $99 - 95 = 4 + 1 = 5$ pages with 2 digits. So, we need $5 \times 2 = 10$ digits.

Next, find the number of pages with 3 digits, that is, pages 100 through 112. Compute: $112 - 100 = 12 + 1 = 13$ pages. We need $13 \times 3 = 39$ digits.
Add: $10 + 39 = 49$ digits total.

10 BIRTHDAY

Carmen's birthday in 2017 was Friday, September 1. On what day was her birthday in 2022?

HINTS

a. How many days in a regular year?

b. How many days in a leap year?

c. How many weeks in a year?

10 BIRTHDAY

Carmen's birthday in 2017 was Friday, September 1. On what day was her birthday in 2022?

SOLUTION 1

a. How many days from September 1, 2017 until September 1, 2018? 365

b. How many weeks in 365? 365 ÷ 7 = 52 weeks with one day left over. So, September 1, 2018 is on a Saturday.

c. How many days from September 1, 2017 until September 1, 2018? 365.

   365 = 52 weeks + 1 day.

d. September 1, 2019 is on a Sunday.

e. How many days from September 1, 2019 to September 1, 2020? 366 (2020 is a leap year).

   366 = 52 weeks + 2 days.

f. September 1, 2020 is not a Monday but it is a Tuesday.

g. September 1, 2021 is a Wednesday.

   Answer: September 1, 2022 is a **Thursday**.

SOLUTION 2

Number of years from 2017 to 2022 = 5 years.

Each year the same date advances one day on regular years of 365 days.

On a leap year, the same date advances two days.

The 5 years from 2017 to 2022 include one leap year, so the advance is 4 + 2 = 6 days ahead from Friday.

Answer: That is a **Thursday**.

11 CLIMBING STEPS

There are 10 steps leading up to the front of Cranbury Town Hall. A large sign posted next to the steps reads:

Climb the steps by taking 1 or 2 steps at a time.

How many ways can you climb the 10 steps?

HINTS

Here are a few ways:
1 + 1 + 1 + 1 + ... = 10
2 + 2 + 2 + 2 + ... = 10
1 + 2 + 1 + 2 + 1 + 2 + 1 = 10
2 + 1 + 2 + 1 + 2 + 1 + 1 = 10

Make it easier: Shrink to 4 steps and look for a pattern.

11 CLIMBING STEPS

There are 10 steps leading up to the front of Cranbury Town Hall. A large sign posted next to the steps reads:

Climb the steps by taking 1 or 2 steps at a time.

How many ways can you climb the 10 steps?

SOLUTION

Make the problem simpler – look for a pattern.
How many ways to climb if there is only 1 step? Answer is 1 way.
For 2 steps: 1 + 1 and 2. Answer is 2 ways.
For 3 steps: 1 + 1 + 1, 2 + 1, and 1 + 2. Answer is 3 ways.
For 4 steps: 1 + 1 + 1 + 1, 2 + 2, 1 + 2 + 1, 2 + 1 + 1, and 1 + 1 + 2. Answer is 5 ways.
Here is what we have so far:

Number of steps	Number of ways
1	1
2	2
3	3
4	5
5	
6	
7	
8	
9	
10	

Do you see a pattern in the number of ways?
There are 8 ways for 5 steps.
The pattern is "add the 2 numbers that come before."
So, 6 steps will be 5 + 8 = 13 ways.
Keep going with this pattern in the table.
Answer: For 10 steps, there are **89** ways.

12 LICENSE PLATE

Wayne's mother just got a new license plate for her car. The plate has five digits, no letters. She asked Wayne to place the license plate on her car. When Wayne placed the plate on her car, he turned the plate upside down (rotated 180 degrees). But there were still five digits!

The difference between the flipped number on the plate and the actual number is 63,783. What is the actual number of the license plate?

HINTS

Which digits can you flip and still see a digit?
Start with 0. What other numbers flip?
What digit do you see when you flip each?
What is the subtraction setup you need to use to solve this?

___ ___ ___ ___ ___   number on the plate (rotated ½ turn)

−

___ ___ ___ ___ ___   actual number

      6   3   7   8   3

12 LICENSE PLATE

Wayne's mother just got a new license plate for her car. The plate has five digits, no letters. She asked Wayne to place the license plate on her car. When Wayne placed the plate on her car, he turned the plate upside down (rotated 180 degrees). But there were still five digits!

The difference between the flipped number on the plate and the actual number is 63,783. What is the actual number of the license plate?

SOLUTION

These are still digits when they are flipped: 0, 1, 6, 8, 9.
Here is the subtraction setup that you must figure out:

___ ___ ___ ___ ___ flipped digits on the plate

−

___ ___ ___ ___ ___ actual digits on the plate

   6   3   7   8   3

How can we get a 3 in the ones place? Remember, digits in the ones place will flip to the ten-thousands place. 9 and 6 can work in the ones place, but 6 and 9 will not work in the ten-thousands place. How about 1 and 8 in the ones place? They become 8 and 1 in the ten-thousands place. That could work.

Answer:

    8 0 6 9 1
    -1 6 9 0 8 actual license plate
    6 3 7 8 3

13 WRITING PAGES IN A BOOK

Ahmad is reading a book that has no page numbers. So, he took out his pen and wrote the page numbers: 1, 2, 3, and so forth. When he finished, he counted the digits he wrote in the book. Digits are 0, 1, 2, 3, 4, 5, 6, 7, 8, 9. He used 642 digits. How many pages are in Ahmad's book?

Note: page 45 has 2 digits, page 105 has 3.

HINTS

How many digits for the first 9 pages?
How many digits for pages 10 through 99?
How many digits for pages 1 through 99?
How many more digits are left, starting with page 100?

13 WRITING PAGES IN A BOOK

Ahmad is reading a book that has no page numbers. So, he took out his pen and wrote the page numbers: 1, 2, 3, and so forth. When he finished, he counted the digits he wrote in the book. Digits are 0, 1, 2, 3, 4, 5, 6, 7, 8, 9. He used 642 digits. How many pages are in Ahmad's book?

Note: page 45 has 2 digits, page 105 has 3.

SOLUTION

Repeating from **HINTS**:

How many digits for the first 9 pages? 9

How many digits for pages 10 through 99? 180

How many digits for pages 1 through 99? 9 + 180 = 189

How many more digits are left, starting with page 100? 642 – 189 = 453

How many digits do we need to write each page number starting with 100? 3

Each page number starting from 100 requires 3 digits, so divide: 453 ÷ 3 = 151, the number of pages starting from page 100.

Add: 99 + 151 = 250

Answer: 250 pages in the book.

14 BUILDING A FENCE

The Parnell family is building a fence around a vegetable garden. The garden is in the shape of a rectangle 12 feet long and 6 feet wide. If they place posts every 2 feet, how many posts will they need?

HINTS

Use this diagram to help solve this problem. Mark the posts.
How many posts along the 6-foot side?
How many posts along the 12-foot side?
Make sure to count the posts on the 4 corners.

14 BUILDING A FENCE

The Parnell family is building a fence around a vegetable garden. The garden is in the shape of a rectangle 12 feet long and 6 feet wide. If they place posts at the corners and 2 feet apart, how many posts will they need?

SOLUTION

Count: 12-foot side: Start with 1 corner post and add 5 more posts. That is 6 posts. Another 6 posts for the second 6-foot side. Total: 2 × 6 = 12

Count: 6-foot side: Start with 1 corner post and add 2 more posts. That is 3 posts. Another 3 posts for the second 3-foot side. Total: 2 × 3 = 6

Add: 12 + 6 = 18

Answer: 18 posts

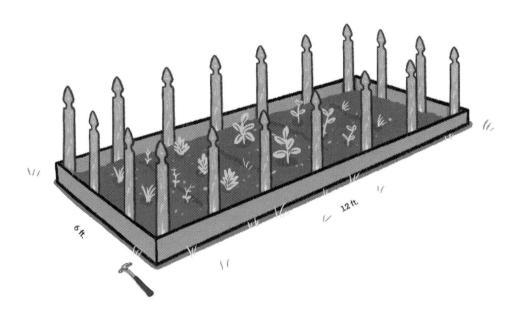

15 MISSING DIGITS

$$A\ B\ C\ D\ E$$
$$\underline{\times\ 4}$$
$$E\ D\ C\ B\ A$$

A, B, C, D, and E stand for digits. Find the digits for each letter.

HINTS

Different letters mean that the digits will be different.

Can A or E = 0?

Do the math: In the ones place, 4 × E = A and in the ten-thousands place, 4 × A = E

Recognize that E in the answer < 10. So, can A = 9? Can A = 8? Can A = 7?

Is A in the answer even or odd?

What is A?

Once you know A, find E.

15 MISSING DIGITS

$$\begin{array}{r} A\ B\ C\ D\ E \\ \times\ 4 \\ \hline E\ D\ C\ B\ A \end{array}$$

A, B, C, D, and E stand for digits. Find the digits for each letter.

SOLUTION

A cannot = 9, 8, 7, 6, 5, 4, or 3. Why? (Answer is a 5-digit number)
Digit A in the answer must be an even number. Why? (Multiplying E by even number)
A must = 2.
So, E is 8. (4 × 8 = 3<u>2</u>)
Check E in the ten-thousands place of the answer: Since E = 8 and since there is no regrouping in the thousands place, B = 1. (If B = 3, then 4 × 3 = 12, regroup 1 to the ten-thousands place will not work.)
So far, we have ABCDE = 21CD8 and EDCBA = 8DC12.
Next, what must D = ? Since B = 1 in the tens place of the answer, D must = 7 because 4 × 7 = 28 + 3 = 31, write 1 for B, and regroup 3. And finally, find C is in the hundreds places of both AB<u>C</u>DE and ED<u>C</u>BA. So, try C = 9 (4 × <u>9</u> = 36 + 3 = 3<u>9)</u> in the hundreds places of both AB<u>C</u>DE and ED<u>C</u>BA).

Answer: AB<u>C</u>DE = 21978

16 STRINGS THAT TELL TIME

You have two strings. Each string takes an hour to burn after you light one end with a match. The strings burn unevenly when you light them. Sometimes they burn quickly, sometimes slower. Using both strings and matches, how can you find out when 15 minutes has passed?

HINTS

How long does it take for a string to burn after you light a match? How long does it take for a string to burn if you light both ends at the same time?

16 STRINGS THAT TELL TIME

You have two strings. Each string takes an hour to burn after you light one end with a match. The strings burn unevenly when you light them. Sometimes they burn quickly, sometimes slower. Using both strings and matches, how can you find out when 15 minutes has passed?

SOLUTION

How long does it take for a string to burn after you light a match? How long does it take a string to burn if you light both ends at the same time?

When you light both ends of a string at the same time, it will take half an hour for the string to burn out.

Answer: Light *both* ends of one string and light *one* end of the second string all at the same time. When the first string burns out, light a match to the other end of the second string.

17 TRAVELING IN GRID CITY

In Malcolm's town, all the streets form squares. Here is part of his town:

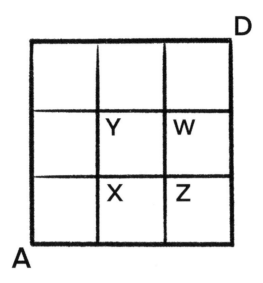

In Grid City, you must travel on roads in a special way. Here are the rules:

a. **You must travel in only two directions: to the right and up.**

b. **You cannot travel down and to the left.**

How many different routes can you take from A to D?

HINTS

How many routes from A to X?
How many routes from A to Y?
How many routes from A to Z?
How many routes from A to W?

17 TRAVELING IN GRID CITY

In Malcolm's town, all the streets form squares. Here is part of his town:

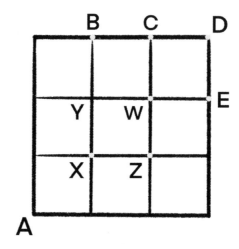

In Grid City, you must travel on roads in a special way. Here are the rules:

a.   **You must travel in only two directions: to the right and up.**

b.   **You cannot travel down and to the left.**

How many different routes can you take from A to D?

SOLUTION

How many routes from A to X? 2
How many routes from A to Y? 3
How many routes from A to Z? 3
There are 3 routes from A to Y and 3 routes to Z.
How many routes are there from A to W?
Add 3 + 3 = 6 routes. Do you see why we add?
From A to B? 4
From A to C? 10
From A to E? 10
<u>**Answer: 20 routes from A to D**</u>

18 COUNTING RECTANGLES

2   2   2   2   2   2   2   2   2   2   2   2   2

1 [   ] 1

Each of the smallest rectangles measures 2 units long and 1 unit wide.
How many rectangles are there altogether?

HINTS

How many 2 by 1 rectangles?
What are the length and width of the next bigger rectangle?
How many rectangles of those dimensions?

18 COUNTING RECTANGLES

Each of the smallest rectangles measures 2 units long and 1 unit wide.

How many rectangles are there altogether?

SOLUTION

Add rows to the table. Then fill in the rest of this table and add.

Length and Width	How many rectangles?
2 by 1	13
4 by 1	12
6 by 1	11
8 by 1	10
10 by 1	
12 by 1	
26 by 1	1

Answer: 91

19 MOVING ALONG A CHECKERBOARD

A checkerboard has 8 rows and 8 columns. A checker moves forward by following a diagonal path. It cannot move backwards along the path.

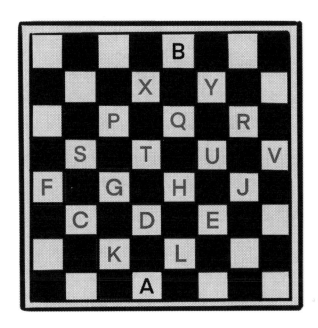

How many different routes are there from A to B?

HINTS

See letters in squares where checker A can move.

Work upwards from the start to locations X and Y.

How many routes are possible from A to get to K? 1

From A to L? 1

From A to D? 1 + 1 = 2

Continue to move forward towards B. Soon you will see a pattern.

19 MOVING ALONG A CHECKERBOARD

A checkerboard has 8 rows and 8 columns. A checker moves forward by following a diagonal path. It cannot move backwards along the path.

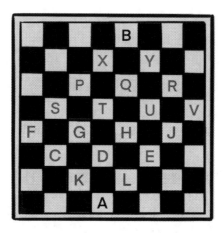

How many different routes are there from A to B?

SOLUTION

See the letters in the squares where checker A can move.
Work upwards from the start to locations X and Y.
How many routes are possible from A to get to K? 1
From A to L? 1
From A to D? 1 + 1 = 2
From A to E? 1
From A to H? 2 + 1 = 3
From A to C? 1
From A to G? 1 + 2 = 3
From A to T? 3 + 3 = 6
Continue in this fashion: from A to U? 3 + 1 = 4
From A to S? 1 + 3 = 4
From A to P? 4 + 6 = 10
To Q? 6 + 4 = 10
To X? 10 + 10 = 20
To R? 4 + 1 = 5
To Y? 5 + 10 = 15
Answer: 20 + 15 = 35 different routes from A to B.

20 COMPLETING A MAGIC SQUARE

6		
		9
	3	

In a magic square the sums of all rows, columns, and the two main diagonals are equal. The digits 1 through 9 can be used once and only once. Fill in the six empty squares to end up with a magic square.

HINTS

The digits 3, 6, and 9 are already used.
Think: What digit is the best for the center square?
Fill in the squares by using trial and error.
Or think about the sum of each row, column, and diagonal.

20 COMPLETING A MAGIC SQUARE

6		
		9
	3	

In a magic square the sums of all rows, columns, and the two main diagonals are equal. The digits 1 through 9 can be used once and only once. Fill in the six empty squares to end up with a magic square.

SOLUTION

The digits are 1, 2, 3, 4, 5, 6, 7, 8, 9.
Which digit is in the middle? It is 5.
Add the digits 1 through 9: the sum is 45
The sums of all 3 columns or rows are equal.
So, we divide: $45 \div 3 = 15$. The sum of each column, row, and diagonal equals 15.

Answer:

6	7	2
1	5	9
8	3	4

It's magic!

21 ADDING ODD NUMBERS

Find a way to find the sum of the first 35 odd numbers: 1 + 3 + 5 + 7 + ... without having to add the numbers one by one.

HINTS

Look for a pattern.
Simplify the problem: add the first 2 odd numbers, then add the first 3 odd numbers, then 4.
$1 + 3 = 4$
$1 + 3 + 5 = 9$
$1 + 3 + 5 + 7 = 16$
What do you see?
Make a table.

21 ADDING ODD NUMBERS

Find a way to find the sum of the first 35 odd numbers: 1 + 3 + 5 + 7 + ... without having to add the numbers one by one.

SOLUTION

1 + 3 = 4
1 + 3 + 5 = 9
1 + 3 + 5 + 7 = 16
Do you see a pattern?
1 + 3 + 5 + 7 + 9 = ?

Add these odd numbers	How many added?	Sum
1 + 3	2	4
1 + 3 + 5	3	9
1 + 3 + 5 + 7	4	16
1 + 3 + 5 + 7 + 9	5	25
1 + 3 + 5 + 7 + 9 + 11	6	36

How many numbers are added when you add the first 35 odd numbers?
What is the sum? **35 × 35**

Answer: 35 × 35 = 1,225

22 COOKING WITH SAND TIMERS

You are following a recipe that reads: cook for 15 minutes. There are two sand timers in the kitchen. One is for 7 minutes and the other is for 11 minutes.

How can you use the two sand timers to get 15 minutes?

HINTS

If you use the sand timers one after the other, how much time does that take?
If you turn over the 11-minute sand timer at the same time as the 7-minute sand timer, how much time is left in the 11-minute sand timer?

22 COOKING WITH SAND TIMERS

You are following a recipe that reads: cook for 15 minutes. There are two sand timers in the kitchen. One is for 7 minutes and the other is for 11 minutes.

How can you use the two sand timers to get 15 minutes?

SOLUTION

If you turn over the 11-minute sand timer at the same time as the 7-minute sand timer, how much time is left in the 11-minute sand timer? 4 minutes

Answer: Turn over both sand timers at the same time. When the 7-minute timer is empty, start cooking. There are 4 minutes left in the 11-minute timer. So, when the 11-minute timer is empty, turn over that timer for 11 minutes more: **4 + 11 = 15 minutes**.

23 TOSSING TWO CUBES

Start with two cubes with all six faces blank.

Which digits can you write on the faces so that when you toss the cubes the probability of getting the numbers 1 through 12 is the same?

HINTS

How many faces on each cube?

There are 10 digits: 0, 1, 2, 3, 4, 5, 6, 7, 8, 9.

How many results are possible when you toss two cubes, including repeats?

The problem requires that each of the results 1, 2, 3, 4, 5, 6, 7, 8, 9, 10, 11, 12 will be equal.

Since each cube has 6 faces, the number of possibilities when you roll two cubes is $6 \times 6 = 36$.

The 36 possibilities include repeats such as $1 + 0$, $1 + 0$, $1 + 0$ when 1, 1, 1 are on three faces of the first cube and 0 is on one face of the second cube.

23 TOSSING TWO CUBES

Start with two cubes with all six faces blank.

What digits can you write on the faces so that when you toss the cubes the probability of getting the numbers 1 through 12 is the same?

SOLUTION

The results will be 1, 2, 3, 4, 5, 6, 7, 8, 9, 10, 11, 12.
All these results will come up equally.
Since each cube has 6 faces, the number of possibilities when you roll two cubes is $6 \times 6 = 36$.
If each of 1 through 12 comes up equally, then each number appears 3 times.
1: 3 times
2: 3 times
3: 3 times
......
12: 3 times

The 36 possibilities include repeats such as $1 + 0, 1 + 0, 1 + 0$ when 1, 1, 1, are on three faces of the first cube and 0 is on one face of the second cube (see table below).

Answer:

Faces of cubes

First cube	Second cube
1	0
1	1
1	2
7	3
7	4
7	5

Note that 12 comes up three times as $7 + 5$, since 7 is on three faces of the first cube.
11 comes up three times as $7 + 4$, since 7 is on three faces of the first cube. And so on, until $1 + 0$ comes up three times.

24 HOW MANY WAYS?

The Cool Cats and the City Slickers will meet in the first round of Big City Soccer Tournament. In this round, it is 3 out of 5 wins. That means the first team to win three games is the winner. How many ways can this round end?

HINTS

Use a table.
Think, three straight wins.
Then one loss.
Then two losses.
Complete one team, then do the other team the same way.

24 HOW MANY WAYS?

The Cool Cats and the City Slickers will meet in the first round of Big City Soccer Tournament. In this round, it is 3 out of 5 wins. That means the first team to win three games is the winner. How many ways can this round end?

SOLUTION

List carefully in a table.
Team wins 3 straight games: CCC and SSS.
Team wins first game and loses 3 straight games.
Team wins second game and loses the other 3 games.
Team loses the third game and wins the other three games.
Continue with all combinations of team losing 2 games and winning 3 games.

C wins	S wins
CCC	SSS
SCCC	CSSS
CSCC	SCSS
CCSC	SSCS
SSCCC	CCSSS
CSSCC	SCCSS
CCSSC	SSCCS
CSCSC	SCSCS
SCSCC	CSCSS
SCCSC	CSSCS

Answer: 20 ways

25 IS THIS SHARING?

In how many ways can three people divide 15 cupcakes so that each person gets at least one cupcake?

HINTS

Make this problem simpler.
Simpler means reducing the number of cupcakes.
Then look for a pattern.

25 IS THIS SHARING?

In how many ways can three people divide 15 cupcakes so that each person gets at least one cupcake?

SOLUTION

Do the numbers in a chart and start with 3 cupcakes.
For 3 cupcakes, each person gets 1.
You can divide 4 cupcakes this way: 1-1-2, 1-2-1, 2-1-1: that is 3 ways.
You can divide 5 cupcakes this way: 2-2-1, 1-2-2, 2-1-2, 3-1-1, 1-3-1, 1-1-3: 6 ways.
You can divide 6 cupcakes this way: 2-2-2, 2-1-3, 1-3-2, 1-2-3, 2-3-1, 3-2-1, 3-1-2, 4-1-1, 1-4-1, 1-1-4: 10 ways.

# Cupcakes	# Ways
3	1
4	3
5	6
6	10
7	?
8	?
9	?

Notice the pattern in the second column: $3 - 1 = \underline{2}$, $6 - 3 = \underline{3}$, $10 - 6 = \underline{4}$. The differences between the numbers increase by 1, so the next number is $10 + \underline{5} = 15$, then it's $15 + \underline{6} = 21$.

Answer: Continue along this way and you will find that there are **91 ways for 3 people to share 15 cupcakes**.

Try It! Math Problems for All

Photocopiable Problems

What follows are photocopiable versions of all 25 problems. These can be copied and used in group settings or used as handouts where access to a student workbook is unavailable.

DOI: 10.4324/9781003406594-2

1 ADDING COINS TO A DOLLAR

a. Show how 50 US coins can add up to one dollar. Use pennies, nickels, dimes, and quarters.

b. Can you find another way to do this?

2 COUNTING HANDSHAKES

a. You are one of ten students in an art class. If everyone shakes hands with everyone else, how many handshakes would there be?

b. If 20 students are in the class, how many handshakes would there be?

3 PHONE

This is part of the keypad of a phone:

The numbers 3-2-7-6 spell the word FARM.

a. What numbers spell PURPLE?

**b. What word do the numbers 6-2-8-4 spell?
Can you get two words?**

4 SQUARES ON A CHECKERBOARD

How many squares are there in an 8 by 8 grid?

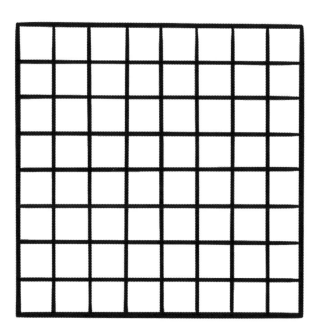

5 CUTTING A ROUND CAKE

Cut a round cake into eight equal parts with three cuts.

61

6 SHARING DONUTS

You and two friends have six donuts. In how many ways can you divide the six donuts so that each person gets at least one donut?

7 BACKWARDS AND FORWARDS

Write a five-letter word that spells the same word backwards and forwards.

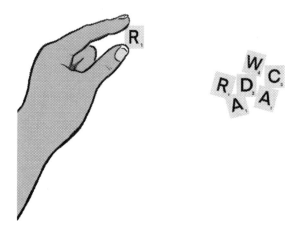

8 HOW MUCH IS YOUR NAME WORTH?

Suppose A = $1, B = $2, C = $3, D = $4, and so forth.

Write your first name here. _____

How much is it worth? _____

Find a name equal to exactly $48.

9 COUNTING DIGITS IN A BOOK

The digits are 0, 1, 2, 3, 4, 5, 6, 7, 8, 9.

We write page numbers with digits: page 42, page 143.

a. **How many digits do we need to write for all pages from page 18 to page 32, including both pages 18 and 32?**

b. **How many digits do we need to write for all the pages from page 95 to page 112, including both page 95 and page 112?**

10 BIRTHDAY

Carmen's birthday in 2017 was Friday, September 1. On what day was her birthday in 2022?

11 CLIMBING STEPS

There are 10 steps leading up to the front of Cranbury Town Hall. A large sign posted next to the steps reads:

Climb the steps by taking 1 or 2 steps at a time.

How many ways can you climb the 10 steps?

12 LICENSE PLATE

Wayne's mother just got a new license plate for her car. The plate has five digits, no letters. She asked Wayne to place the license plate on her car. When Wayne placed the plate on her car, he turned the plate upside down (rotated 180 degrees). But there were still five digits!

The difference between the flipped number on the plate and the actual number is 63,783. What is the actual number of the license plate?

13 WRITING PAGES IN A BOOK

Ahmad is reading a book that has no page numbers. So, he took out his pen and wrote the page numbers: 1, 2, 3, and so forth. When he finished, he counted the digits he wrote in the book. Digits are 0, 1, 2, 3, 4, 5, 6, 7, 8, 9. He used 642 digits. How many pages are in Ahmad's book?

Note: page 45 has 2 digits, page 105 has 3.

14 BUILDING A FENCE

The Parnell family is building a fence around a vegetable garden. The garden is in the shape of a rectangle 12 feet long and 6 feet wide. If they place posts every 2 feet, how many posts will they need?

15 MISSING DIGITS

$$A\ B\ C\ D\ E$$
$$\times\ 4$$
$$\overline{E\ D\ C\ B\ A}$$

A, B, C, D, and E stand for digits. Find the digits for each letter.

16 STRINGS THAT TELL TIME

You have two strings. Each string takes an hour to burn after you light one end with a match. The strings burn unevenly when you light them. Sometimes they burn quickly, sometimes slower. Using both strings and matches, how can you find out when 15 minutes has passed?

17 TRAVELING IN GRID CITY

In Malcolm's town, all the streets form squares. Here is part of his town:

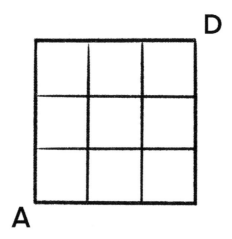

In Grid City, you must travel on roads in a special way. Here are the rules:

a. You must travel in only two directions: to the right and up.

b. You cannot travel down and to the left.

How many different routes can you take from A to D?

18 COUNTING RECTANGLES

2 2 2 2 2 2 2 2 2 2 2 2 2

1 [   ] 1

Each of the smallest rectangles measures 2 units long and 1 unit wide.

How many rectangles are there altogether?

19 MOVING ALONG A CHECKERBOARD

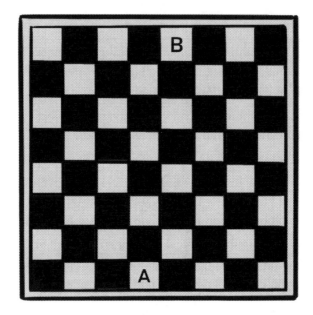

A checkerboard has 8 rows and 8 columns. A checker moves forward by following a diagonal path. It cannot move backwards along the path.

How many different routes are there from A to B?

20 COMPLETING A MAGIC SQUARE

6		
		9
	3	

In a magic square the sums of all rows, columns, and the two main diagonals are equal. The digits 1 through 9 can be used once and only once. Fill in the six empty squares to end up with a magic square.

21 ADDING ODD NUMBERS

Find a way to find the sum of the first 35 odd numbers: 1 + 3 + 5 + 7 + ... without having to add the numbers one by one.

22 COOKING WITH SAND TIMERS

You are following a recipe that reads: cook for 15 minutes. There are two sand timers in the kitchen. One is for 7 minutes and the other is for 11 minutes.

How can you use the two sand timers to get 15 minutes?

23 TOSSING TWO CUBES

Start with two cubes with all six faces blank.

What digits can you write on the faces so that when you toss the cubes the probability of getting the numbers 1 through 12 is the same?

24 HOW MANY WAYS?

The Cool Cats and the City Slickers will meet in the first round of Big City Soccer Tournament. In this round, it is 3 out of 5 wins. That means the first team to win three games is the winner. How many ways can this round end?

25 IS THIS SHARING?

In how many ways can three people divide 15 cupcakes so that each person gets at least one cupcake?

About the Author

Dr. Kaplan is Professor Emeritus of Mathematics Education at Seton Hall University. Previously, he taught first grade and high school in New York City. Later, Jerry was Associate Professor at Teachers College, Columbia University, and Visiting Professor at the University of Tel Aviv, Israel. He has conducted research and written widely on many areas of teaching and learning mathematics, applying research to the practical needs of the mathematics curriculum and classroom.

Among his many interests in education, one stands out – the role of problem solving activities that combine more than one area of the school's curriculum. Call it cross–curriculum problem solving. In spite of the efforts of Jerry and others, he admits that this area has not caught on, but thinks the time is now ripe for problem solving.

Jerry designed and wrote special books for **Triumph Learning** to help students prepare for state and national tests. These books, all bearing the title "**Coach**", are tailored to students who have difficulty with math and math tests.

He has led many workshops, seminars, and classes on how to implement problem solving into new curricula. He always encourages teachers to reach beyond the ordinary to include problem solving and non-standard experiences for their students.

Several beneficiaries of his work in these areas have been the Job Corps Program, the Ford Foundation, the Educational Testing Service, and the Ministry of Education, Israel.

He is a co-author of a set of books for McGraw-Hill, a major textbook series for Harcourt School Publishers, high school texts for Science Research Associates (SRA), and a management learning system for Random House.

About the Illustrator

Ysemay Dercon is a freelance illustrator and graduate of the Rhode Island School of Design. She is currently based in Providence, Rhode Island. Her creative pursuits lie in the worlds of publishing, art and science communication, portraiture, and journalistic illustration. She strives to create art that communicates about the world around us in a meaningful and engaging way. You can find her work in books such as *The Little Gardener. Helping Children Connect with the Natural World*, a primer on gardening meant for both children and adults, published by Princeton Architectural Press. She has also worked closely with Osa Conservation, a non-profit conservation and research organization located in the Osa Peninsula of Costa Rica. Her collaboration with Osa Conservation involved creating the illustrations for a series of interpretive panels that have been installed on the trail system of the organization's property. When not creating, she enjoys going for long walks outdoors, reading memoirs, and spending time in cafes with friends.

Printed in the United States
by Baker & Taylor Publisher Services